PRAISE
Orientation to G...

"The best advice for someone en...
journey often comes from those who have recently experienced a similar challenge or opportunity. Austin and Savannah's unique combination of experience provides personal, yet professional advice on all spectrums of the college experience that I would recommend to any upcoming or current students. I wish I would have had such a well-organized guide available to me before I entered college!"

CARL REAM
Supply Chain Lead, Steelcase Inc.
Michigan State University '13

"I love this book... I buy it for each of my kids as they turn 18. It's great advice that gives young people a head start on their college experience... Plus Savannah and Austin have a great way of weaving truth and experience into great stories"

CHRIS ELMORE
Co-Founder, AvidXchange
UNC-Charlotte '93

"This book is something I wish I read before I went to college. The "straight talk" and simple action steps that you suggested would be incredibly helpful to any incoming freshman. It is clear the genuine passion that

Savannah had for her university, friends, and experiences she had attending college. Every student should have the opportunity to make the most of their college career and have these lifelong memories just like Savannah and Austin. This book will help put you in a position to make these lifelong memories."

Chad Howard
Account Executive, Procter and Gamble
Drake University '14

Austin and Savannah have done an outstanding job in capturing their own unique college experiences, and finding ways to offer up simple, relevant, and very helpful suggestions for matriculating students to prepare to make the most of their own college journeys. While not a playbook for college, their ability to deconstruct and demystify the challenging, and often complex, transition from high school to college, and from teenager to adult, makes *Orientation to Graduation 2.0* a must have for any student heading to campus, and a great reference while there. Having been a professor for 16 years, I know many of my students could have benefited from this resource. And furthermore, with my first child on the way to college this Fall, and two more following in the next three years (yes, 3 in college at the same time at one point!), this will be REQUIRED reading.

Chip Snively
Professor, UNC-Chapel Hill
University of Kentucky, '85
Indiana University, MBA '91

Orientation to Graduation 2.0 is an excellent read for students beginning their college journey! This book touches on various situations and preparations throughout the college journey. Well done!

KEVIN ALLMAN
Gear Up Coordinator, Swain County Schools
Western Carolina University '93

After way too much information about what to do to get INTO college, this book is a must read on what to expect when you get there. Austin and Savannah share their personal experiences and offer great suggestions for students everywhere.   Easy to read, witty.... you will feel like they are your best friends when you finish.

LISA KLOSTER
CFO, Pace Harmon
UNC-Chapel Hill '85

Austin & Savannah are rare breeds. Like kind over-achievers will feel a sense of relief in that they can stay the course and successfully navigate college. The majority of kids that are less motivated should read this in 9th grade!

MIKE GRIFFIN
Partner, Griffin Brothers Companies
UNC-Chapel Hill '87

"This is the perfect book with real live experiences rather than the perspective of someone who is quite removed from the college experience. Austin and Savannah provide a truthful insight into the life of a college student while offering professional advice based on those situations. I wish I had access to a book like this when I entered college as it is an amazing guide for all types of students."

CHIP PALMER, Ph.D.
Learning Assistance Coordinator, Pfeiffer University
Pfeiffer University '09, UNCC '11, Walden University '18

"This book should be required summer reading for any incoming college freshman interested in succeeding in both college and life. The advice that Austin and Savannah offer on how college students can make the most of their time in college is invaluable, especially goal setting, time management, getting out of your comfort zone, and being willing to fail in order to grow. I'll definitely be giving a copy of *Orientation to Graduation 2.0* to my 15-year old daughter when she graduates high school.

GARY PARKER, CFA
Managing Director,
GreerWalker Corporate Finance
University of Florida '86

"Knowledge and experiences are a huge part of what makes a person. Austin and Savannah do a fantastic job of providing tips, tricks, and best practices for the one time in your life, college, where your knowledge and experiences are expanded constantly. To compliment the tips and tricks, the real-life stories make the book relatable and downright honest."

CHRISTOPHER DONALDSON
Senior Consultant, IBM
UNC-Chapel Hill Class of '16

"Savannah and Austin have teamed up to create a dialogue that is REAL and REFRESHING. The authors' bravery for telling their own personal stories creates a sense of trust with the reader unlike any other guide I've read. I will be recommending this to all my little cousins entering college these next few years!"

PAIGE NEUENFELDT
EY Customer Consultant
UNC Chapel Hill '16

Orientation to Graduation 2.0 is a must read for undergrads of all ages. Whether an entering freshman or a rising junior, Savannah and Austin's advice for navigating the social, educational, and professional challenges of higher education are targeted and easy -to-implement. Professors could easily utilize a combination of chapter activities and to-do-lists to facilitate college success focused active learning in the classroom.

DR. NATALIE EDWARDS BISHOP
Associate Dean of the Library &
First Year Experience Professor
Gardner-Webb University

"Orientation to Graduation 2.0 is a must have gift for all future college students. I absolutely love the "our two cents" at the end of each chapter that provides quick takeaways. The dialogue format causes you to feel like you are sitting in the middle of the sofa with Austin and Savannah as they explain to you the do's and don'ts of college. This book will help any college student save money, time, and plenty of headaches!"

CHERESA SIMPSON, PH.D.
Assistant Professor, North Carolina Central University
North Carolina A&T State University '10

Very practical advice that is grounded in the realities of college life. I truly appreciated the perspectives that were shared, and the summaries provided at the end of the chapters - "Our Two Cents". This book is a gem for future or current college students. The advice and perspectives provided in Orientation to Graduation 2.0 can be shared with future students, their parents, and those that work in higher education or prepare students for their future in higher education. This book is relatable to incoming freshman I teach at Queens University – so I will be sharing Austin and Savannah's advice and their "Two Cents."

GINGER BLACK
Assistant Professor Cato School of Education
Queens University of Charlotte

As a mom of two fairly recent college graduates, I can only comment positively on the information that Orientation to Graduation 2.0 provides to all the students entering their new world known as college. Austin and Savannah's insights into so many different aspects of college is phenomenal. Not only are their own experiences insightful and full of great information, but the suggestions they make for students to make the most of the college experience is spot on. These four years (sometimes more) usually prove to be the students' most exciting years to date. This book is written from the heart with warmth, honesty and a sense of humor. This book is an excellent tool for any college student and should motivate them to make the most of their college experience; wherever they choose to attend.

JAN MILLER
Self Employed in Pharmacy Specialty Services
Drake University '83

"I felt as though I was sitting down with Austin and Savannah as they recounted their college experiences. Orientation to Graduation contains key advice straight from the source that is useful to anyone making the exciting and challenging transition into college. Each chapter guides you through every emotion and experience throughout the college journey and I certainly wish I had a guide like this to help navigate my own college career!"

GRACE RADLER
Investor Relations Associate, Ginkgo Residential
Winthrop University '15

A Helms Ventures LLC dba **Oh My Publishing**
3229 Hollyhill Circle
Valdese, NC 28690
www.austinhelms.org

Ordering Information:
Quantity sales. Special discounts are available on quantity purchases by schools, school districts, corporations, and others. For details, contact the publisher at the address above.

Orders by U.S. trade bookstores and wholesalers. Please contact Austin Helms: Tel: (828) 448-5521

Printed in the United States of America
First Edition

Book Design and Typesetting by Stewart A. Williams

Dedication

We'd like to dedicate this book to all of the teachers and professors for challenging, inspiring, and loving us over the years. These special people are the reason we are able to write this book, so all of our gratitude goes to them.

Thank you for being passionate, caring, and loving people!

AUSTIN & SAVANNAH

ORIENTATION

– TO –

GRADUATION

2.0

ADVICE FROM
REAL COLLEGE STUDENTS

AUSTIN HELMS

SAVANNAH PUTNAM

CONTENTS

INTRODUCTION

A New Era of College Guide Books

"A New Perspective"

A: I finished writing the first version of <u>Orientation to Graduation</u> with the thought that I could write one book, tell students to **make the most of their college experience**, and that my writing career would be over. I thought that checking **publish a book** off my goal list would fulfill my mission, and I'd never write again... Well, it turns out, I was wrong and it's only for the better.

Once I published the first edition of this book (May 8th, 2017), I began traveling to high schools and colleges. I've had the opportunity to speak to thousands of students, which has been most enjoyable. I've been able to share the gospel of living for the **oh my** moments, how to make the most of every second of the journey, and that it's okay to fail while in college. Side note: I have also learned that the first version of my book had many typos, but what can I say? I'm just a kid from Valdese.

My first book was an inside look on how I believe

each student can make the most of their college experience. No matter their background, income, hometown, race, you name it - college is a clean slate. It encompassed stories and experiences during my time in college from 2012-2016; it shined a light on the fact that if you write it down and go after it, you can turn your dreams into reality.

Through these presentations, I quickly learned that my version of the college experience was impactful but, it was only **my** perspective. After a few presentations, I had the idea to write a new book, but only if I could find the right person to write it with me. For months I searched for a right fit to add a different perspective and flare to my writing, and as you might guess, that's when Ms. Savannah Putnam's name crossed my mind.

I'm looking forward to reading Savannah's story with you, and trust me, you won't be disappointed. Savannah is filled with ambition, extremely smart, and one of the sweetest people I've ever met. She'll give you her down-right honest opinion on the difficult parts of college, and she'll do so with a different lens than I can.

Orientation to Graduation 2.0 is the beginning of a new era of college guide books. This book was written during Savannah's senior year of college and gives her real-life take on how any student can make the most of their four-year journey. The goal of this book and books that will follow is to find ambitious, successful college students (like Savannah) to tell their stories and share their advice with incoming college students.

I can't imagine doing college without talking to Savannah first. So, without further ado, let me introduce you to the newest college graduate and co-author of *Orientation to Graduation 2.0*, Ms. Savannah Putnam.

S: Hey folks! My name is Savannah Putnam. I'm from a small town in North Carolina called Morganton. I graduated from UNC Chapel Hill in 2019, and I'm heading to law school this fall. I want to go to law school to be a nonprofit lawyer. Being a lawyer will allow me to be people-focused, to educate others, and to serve a variety of communities. This book presents a perfect opportunity for me to educate and serve, just in a little bit of a different way.

Throughout my experience in college and all of the memories I've gathered over the years, I believe that I have made the most of my time here. My differing roles on campus from a recruitment counselor to Student Body President have really opened my eyes about all the world has to teach young people. I can't wait to share with you how my education has had such a profound impact on my life and how I can help you best prepare for the most unique four years of your life.

Ironically enough, it was the day before senior year that Austin asked me to be his co-author for his book. I was nervous, but excited, as I was surrounded by my friends on our front porch talking about what was yet to come. As we were catching up on everyone's summer, we also talked about advice we wish we had known our first-year. In all of our almost-senior-year wisdom, we laughed about the dumb things we had done during our first semester at school. Whether it was going to the wrong class, missing important dates and deadlines, or trying to flirt with the cute kid beside us in class, we talked about our triumphs and failures. Around the same time, I got a notification on my phone from Austin. I had known Austin for several years and had always kept up with him through Facebook likes and Instagram comments. To my surprise, Austin asked me to help co-author this book. The universe seemed to be listening to my conversation and had presented me with an opportunity to make impactful change. With that, I eagerly responded, excited to tackle this challenge.

We are writing to give you all **real** advice on what actually happens in college. It isn't always easy, but it isn't always hard either. We've been there. As much as I love getting advice from people older than me, sometimes they simply don't understand. And as much as I love my parents' well-intentioned wisdom, it isn't always helpful (sorry mom)! Why not take suggestions from real college kids? We will guide you from orientation to graduation with funny narratives about our own experiences and mistakes. College is challenging, but with the right advice, you'll be able to make the most of it!

*ps. We'll distinguish Austin as **A** and Savannah as **S** in the book, so you'll know whose voice is speaking!*

CHAPTER 1

Welcome to College

"Don't forget... XL Twin sheets!"

A: Chances are, if you're reading this book, you're either about to graduate high school, you just graduated, or you're a parent of a student who is interested in what college is all about these days. But, most likely, you're bright-eyed, bushy-tailed, and you can't wait to tackle this thing called college.

College is like a 12'x14' first-year dorm room. You can't fit everything in it, yet you'll try your hardest, too. You'll probably experience it with someone you've never lived with or never met. You'll most likely have to get creative when you purchase the regular (wrong) twin sheets, instead of the XL twin sheets (don't forget this minor, yet important detail – XL Twins are the only ones that fit the tiny dorm bed). Even though you may resent it at first, before long it'll feel like a tiny home – by that time they'll be forcing you out.

You don't want to hear about college from me though;

I'm an old man (24). Savannah knows all about the first days of college.

S: The first day of college is weird. It's that simple.

You're all alone, maybe surrounded with a few friends from your hometown, yet you are accompanied by so many people. After my mom and dad dropped me off I nervously did what I do best: talked to people. I introduced myself to my neighbors and offered my roommates help moving in.

The first few days are packed full of, "Hi nice to meet you!" and "Wait, so where are you from?" You'll remember faces but not names and you'll pass people walking to class not knowing if you should say hello or not. It isn't exactly like what you see in the movies – there aren't parties and college kids going wild on move-in day. But all of the excitement, the buzz of what's to come, is real. Parents and family members are putting on brave faces as they drop off their babies to be on their own for the first time, all while those babies are eagerly waiting for freedom but are also experiencing the fear of being independent.

It's important to remember that everyone is in the same boat as you. No one quite knows what they are doing, and you are all experiencing the same transition from home to somewhere unfamiliar. The first few days you will be challenged to push yourself outside of your comfort zone. There will be unfamiliar topics that you'll talk about, there will be awkward silences followed by uncontrollable laughter. Just remember that everyone is trying just as hard to make friends and to find their place. The best part about going to college is the people you meet and how just three weeks of knowing each other can feel like a lifetime.

College is different... get ready

Take advantage of these next few years because they go by SO quickly. This is an amazing opportunity to find your interests, explore new ideas, and make mistakes.

Our Two Cents

- Get outside of your comfort zone.
- Go meet your neighbors.
- Enjoy every second of the college journey, even the packing process.
- Don't be afraid to make mistakes.

CHAPTER 2

Goal Setting

"Want it so bad your skin will bleed."

A: College consists of three main categories: Academics, Extracurriculars, and Social life. In my experience, most college students can focus, and be very successful, in one or two of these categories at a time. For instance, I never saw a straight-A student partying every night. On the rare occasion I did, I knew that person was spending hours in the library before partying.

During my college journey, I experienced different categories: I was solely focused on academics during my first two years because I knew I wanted to be accepted in the business school on campus. During my junior year I started a business, and my senior year was all about being social. Knowing what your goals are, and what you want to do with your college experience is vital in order to make sure you're focusing on the correct things. If you want to be accepted into medical school, your grades better be superb, but that doesn't mean you can't have friends! It just means your primary focus should be on academics.

Over the past two years, I've had the opportunity to ask high school and college students a simple question: "What would you do if money didn't exist?" The question always creates dialogue, no matter the background of the students, and I am always amazed by the responses. Some of them were, "I'd play Fortnite every day!" "I'd sail around the world!," and, "I'd become a doctor or a dentist." I ask that simple question to prove a point. We all have goals, dreams, and desires, but very few of us verbalize them to other people and even fewer write them down.

Before I made it to move-in day of college, I had a list of goals printed out and laminated. The goals ranged from graduating high school, finding the love of my life, starting a major company, etc. These goals still follow me today, and they acted as a motivators and powerful reminders throughout my college journey.

I was once asked by a college academic professional, Dr. Jim Gulledge of Pfeiffer University, "How are you able to accomplish goals that you write down?" The question stumped me because I had never thought about it; I just wrote things down and did them. After some thought, a realization came across my mind. I'm competitive. Heck, we're all competitive to some extent, and if I wrote down what I hoped to accomplish and showed the world (my Facebook/Instagram friends), I had to at least try to achieve my goals.

So, my challenge to you, especially if you haven't made it to college yet or you're just beginning the journey, is to **pause**. Put your phone down, turn off the WiFi, and get out a piece of paper. Or, on second thought, you really only need an index card and an open mind.

I once read that "If you set your goals high enough, your failure will be above everyone else's success." That quote has always played over and over in my head, especially when trying to define what the word **success** means to each person. Simply put, success to each person means something totally different. However, I believe that if you want to be a **successful** college student, you need to set some goals to know what you're working towards. If it's just to graduate – that's great, or if it's to go to grad school – that's great. Write these goals down to define what success really means to you.

During my junior year of college, one of my professors, Mr. Jim Kitchen, challenged my class to set goals for ourselves with a simple index card (see below). The card required us to make goals in all aspects of our lives (i.e., personal, professional, financial, and family). The goals were all listed on the front of the card, and the back of the card was where we put our biggest dreams, strengths, and areas of interest. My addition to the card was, "what would you do with your life if money if didn't exist." After we filled out the card, we had to fold it up, and place it in our wallets. The card still travels with me everywhere I go and is a simple reminder to always be striving to be the best person I can be in all areas of my life, and to always push to achieve greater heights. Thus, I am dynamically making new cards and goals.

Goal card how-to: Divide the front side of the card into fourths. The topics can differ depending on the person, but most everyone has **Personal, Professional, Financial, and Family goals.** A personal fifth one that I add in is **Faith**! Be very detailed when writing what goals you have, and write about three to five goals for each section. For example, if you want to have kids one day, how many do you want to have? Or, if you want to become a doctor, what type of doctor? Where do you want to go to medical school? The last piece is that these can be 1-5-year goals, or you can extend it to 1-10-year goals. I love 1-5 because by that time you should be a college graduate!

1-5 YEAR GOALS	
Personal Goals	**Professional Goals**
• A personal goal could be: "I want to run in a marathon" • List 2-5 goals • Be as detailed as possible!	• A professional goal could be: "I maintain a job on campus" • List 2-5 goals • Be as detailed as possible!
Financial Goals	**Family Goals**
• A financial goal could be: "I want to be debt free" • List 2-5 goals • Be as detailed as possible!	• A family goal could be: "I want to call home once a week" • List 2-5 goals • Be as detailed as possible!

1-5-YEAR GOALS

What's your dream in life?

What are your strengths?

What are your areas of interest (media, sports, healthcare, etc)?

What would you do with your life if money didn't exist?

On the back of the card write down four titles: What's your dream in life? What are your strengths? What are your areas of interest (media, sports, healthcare, etc)? And finally, the question I ask all of the students I work with, What would you do with your life if money didn't exist?

Now, it's your turn. Write your goals down, and let your imagination take control! Don't be scared of where your goals can take you- and after you write them down, hang em' up! Or at least carry them in your wallet everywhere you go.

S: In order to set a goal, a foundational question has to be answered: what drives you? Is it family? Is it money? Is it the opportunity to help others? Is it to improve yourself or your situation?

For me, I am driven to serve others. I've been afforded countless opportunities throughout my life and I have always had the desire to help others, in whatever way I could.

One example of achieving a goal I set out to do occurred in my junior year. I decided to run for Student

Body President. At my campus, this is no small feat. The election mimicked a real election and sometimes it can get chippy. There were several logistical challenges as I attempted to balance all of my various roles. I was still a student, a friend, a daughter, and an emerging public figure at my university. I quickly realized that it is impossible to make everyone happy. On top of that, I had to help manage a campaign team of around 250 people. It took months of planning outreach strategies and marketing techniques to make sure that the message I wanted to convey was articulated perfectly. I worked incredibly hard during those months. It was exhausting but the end goal is what drove me to continue with the process. I ran an entire campaign around two main concepts: feasible impact and attainable change. Throughout my time in office, the platform goals were completed one by one.

I've applied the feasible and attainable concept to my everyday goal setting. I often find that setting small goals helps me feel more accomplished, productive, and generally happier. Those goals vary drastically but they include things like answering all my emails, running 3 miles that day, or connecting with a friend I haven't seen in a long time.

On the first day of the election, I was out campaigning in 20-degree weather, at 6am and did not leave until about midnight that night. By the end of the day my face was chapped so badly that my skin was bleeding. It was entirely worth it.

After long days and nights of campaigning, I ended

up winning the election and learned a very important lesson: **luck and skill may help you along the way, but hard work and determination will grant you the results you want.** I never wrote down my goals (even though I probably should have- that's great advice, Austin!). I simply found something I wanted and pursued it to all end. I encourage you to do whatever you need to do to get it done... even if it does make your skin bleed!

Our Two Cents

➤ Make short term and long-term goals.
➤ Make attainable goals.
➤ Use resources like college advising, career counseling, and professors to obtain your goals.
➤ Have fun with goal setting. You can never reach too high!
➤ Write em down, print em out, hang em up!

CHAPTER 3

Mistakes and Failures

"Fail Free Zone"

S: Before we get into the nitty-gritty advice, it is so important to recognize that mistakes happen. College isn't going to be a super easy-breezy experience. You will struggle, you will fail, and you will grow.

A: Over the past three years, I've had the opportunity to tell students that there is a place called the "Fail Free Zone." Sounds fake, right? Well, I don't think so, and I'm hoping that Savannah and I can help you see why!

Failure is inevitable. You're going to fail an exam (or do more poorly than you'd like), you're going to mess up a relationship, and you're going to say the wrong thing even if you don't mean to. Chances are you'll fail more times than you'll want. However, the best thing about college is that you're very young and shouldn't have it all figured out. I'm a firm believer that every college should have a sign that says, "Welcome to the Fail-Free Zone!

(where you can fail 100 times, and you'll still have things to try!)"

Savannah and I were both successful college students. Our mistakes and failures helped mold us into the people we have become. However, we didn't become successful college students without failing first. College is a giant playground for you to go try new things, fall on your face if it doesn't work out, and most importantly, a place where you have to learn how to get back on your feet!

S: During my junior year, I applied to a prestigious position on campus. I was selected for an interview. I had thoroughly prepped and came in with an action plan. I thought I did very well but I didn't get the position. I was disappointed, upset, and confused. However, when this door closed, another one opened. This was when I decided I should run for Student Body President. I was able to take a failure and use it as a motivator for another goal. You can't get bogged down by not achieving goals; failure is going to happen. It's important to move forward and set your sights on something new.

There have been numerous other times in my life where I have failed. Sometimes, I have failed to be a good friend. You'll know when you've said or done something that has made another person upset. Occasionally, other people can get upset because you have just failed to listen. In times like this, it is important to reflect and understand why other people may be upset. Realize that their feelings are valid, express validation of how they are feeling, and apologize. Often, we never intentionally upset someone. Just acknowledge that sometimes you mess up, give the other person time to heal, and work to move on together.

College allows you to make mistakes in a healthy environment. Mistakes aren't make or break, they are learning experiences. If you're anything like me, you'll call your mom every time something goes wrong. She will comfort you and put things into perspective. Even when the world feels like it is ending, it isn't. Mistakes happen; learn how to accept it and move on. College, and life, are too short to harp on the past.

Our Two Cents

➤ College allows you to make more mistakes with less consequences, so it's okay to fail. Move on and get back on your feet.

➤ You will fail time and time again. It just matters what you do next!

➤ Fail early! Learn from your mistakes and don't do them again.

CHAPTER 4

Time Management, Support Team, and Homesickness

"Call your mama!"

A: When you move from the comfort of your own home community, where it feels like you know everyone, transitioning to a new place (with new people) is no easy task.

S: It can be overwhelming and frightening. It may be seamless for some and others may take all semester or even the entire first year to finally feel comfortable away from their loved ones.

A: Even though the transition can be tough, I'm hoping we can make it a bit easier for you. We believe there are three main things that you'll either need to learn, build, or be ready for... because they're all coming.

Time Management (learn it)

A: You'll quickly realize that in order to be successful in college, you have to manage your time wisely.

S: During my first year, I quickly learned about time management. I was incredibly eager to get involved and joined every club I could get my hands on. I quickly found myself overwhelmed and didn't have adequate time to do my homework. On top of being involved with too many extracurriculars, one of my professors assigned around 60 pages of reading about the Industrial Revolution every night. Coupled with the assignments from four other classes, I was drowning in homework.

If I was going to be a successful college student, I needed to reassess my workload and schedule. So, I dropped some of the clubs that I knew I wasn't going to be able to dedicate myself to and found a balance. It didn't happen overnight, but I feel like as a college graduate, I have become much more of an expert in time management.

To-do lists do wonders!

S: A big reason that I am able to balance a variety of things is because of the wonderful, yet simple, to-do list. My to-do list is, quite literally, my saving grace. It helps me stay organized and makes sure that I am getting things done when they need to be. I make a little to-do list every morning on a sticky note or a piece of paper. I put it in my pocket and check things off along the way. It is always helpful for me to visualize exactly what I need to do. I highly recommend a little list or something that helps you remember all of the assignments, lunch dates, and emails that you will have to deal with.

The beauty of college (especially during your junior and senior years) is you have control of your class schedule and when you take your classes. During my first year, I front-loaded my week, meaning most of my classes were on Monday's and Wednesday's. Taking most of my classes at the beginning of the week allowed me to get ahead on assignments. Now, if I'm honest, I didn't work ahead on every single one of them, but I did do my best to get ahead. For example, if a paper was due on Friday, I would start working on it on Monday morning and try and have it be complete by Wednesday. I would read over it, edit it if needed, and send it in on the day it was due. I wouldn't wait until Thursday night to start it (I have a friend that does this and it kills me every.single.time.), partly because I am a firm believer in the idea that homework simply cannot be done between Friday afternoon and Sunday morning.

I did my very best to stick to the idea of getting ahead throughout my college career. I planned my day around my classes and would go to the library in between them to work on all of the things I needed to get done. Even if that meant getting up earlier or staying up later than I would have liked, I would always do my best to be done by Friday afternoon. It allowed me to relax and unwind from the week that I had and to be focused and present when I was with my friends.

You will be able to find your own way of managing your time. It will take setbacks and you will struggle at some point, but once you realize that it could have been avoided if you had managed your time better, you will never make the same mistake.

A: If you can master time management during your first few months in college, your life will be much, much easier. Time management can affect your relationships, your classes, landing your first job out of college- you name it. Being able to manage your time while in college shows you have your life together, and that you aren't just going to college for a great time (trust me I had a great time). Managing your time wisely shows that you truly want to make the most of every opportunity that college throws at you.

S: Another time management piece of advice, **don't be late.** While this may be a personal pet peeve of mine, I still think it is important to note. If you are going to be late, at least let the other person know. If you say you're going to be there at 9 o'clock, be there at nine.

A: If you manage your time it shows that you value your time as much as you value someone else's!

Support Team (build it)

S: I have several different support teams at school, which I believe is what has allowed me to thrive. I have my family, which is the foundation. I have my closest friends and I have my sorority sisters (who I truly believe would drop everything for me if I needed them to).

A: Your support team isn't just something you need for college- it's something that you will lean on and rely on for the rest of your life. It's those people that get invited to your wedding (like I said in my last book, I know my future wife is going to kill it with all these invites I have promised people). Your support team is always in your corner, always willing to give you advice, the right kind of advice, and will most likely change over time. Don't forget that if someone is in your support team, then you could also be in theirs, always be willing to give back!

S: Speaking of giving back, you will also be a part of someone's support team. This doesn't mean it's a job or a drop-everything-every-time-they-call kind of deal. It is about being there for people when they need it most. It is about listening, having hard conversations, and acting in their best interest. The first semester of my senior year I was overwhelmed with all of the things I had going on. My job was so demanding, my class schedule was rigorous, I was applying to law schools, and simply felt like I couldn't catch my breath. My friends and family quickly took note of this. They called in and checked on me, brought me candy, and did everything they could to make my life a little bit easier. They were there for me and I'll be there for them, whenever that may be.

Homesickness (be ready for it)

S: The word 'homesickness' is defined differently by different people. For me, I didn't necessarily have homesickness because once I graduated high school, I was ready for something new. I had also just spent a month away from my parents the summer before going to college. However, that didn't necessarily mean my transition to college was the easiest thing to do. I missed my parents. I missed my dogs. I missed my favorite hometown restaurants. It just took time to adjust. You'll get accustomed to the feeling of being on your own and then going home will feel like a treat. It may be seamless for some and others may take all semester or even the year to finally feel comfortable being away from their loved ones.

The single best advice I can give to you in college is to call home. Call your mom, your grandma, your teacher, your friends, anyone who wants to know how you're doing. Call on your walk home or in between classes. It doesn't have to be a chore or a 30-minute conversation. Checking in on those that you love will never go out of style.

A: I found homesickness to be really ironic because I would feel the need to go home and get my mama's loving, yet I was building a new home in college. Looking back, my college town became home. You too will probably experience homesickness, and my way of dealing with it was leaning on my support team and calling home. However, if you're making the most of college, college will become home. You'll fall in love with the people that are around you, your little XL twin bed will begin to feel like the one from your childhood room, and before long, you'll be missing college as if it was home.

Our Two Cents

- ➤ Call your family.
- ➤ Make the best of your new situation.
- ➤ Making friends in college can be easy for some and hard for others. Step out of your comfort zone as early as you can. Making impactful friends is one of the best parts of college and will allow you to create a support network early in your college journey!
- ➤ No matter WHO is in your support team, build a team for you!

CHAPTER 5

Living Arrangements

"THAT'S MY ROOMMATE!"

S: My first year, I lived in a suite style dorm, meaning that there were eight people to one bathroom, four rooms with two people in each room. I always had my own room at my home, but I was constantly sharing a room at basketball tournaments or soccer outings, so I wasn't exactly bothered by the idea of a roommate. Unfortunately, I shared a bathroom with my brother when I was younger, so I figured if I could survive that, I could survive sharing with seven other people.

In that suite, in the room across from mine, is where I found some of my very best friends. I quickly learned that I gravitate towards people who share the same worldview as I do. We all worked hard, played harder, and valued the time we spent together. After a long day, I would walk into their room collapse on the floor and talk and laugh until I was able to get back up. I didn't necessarily have a space in my own dorm room where I could relax and unwind, so their floor was the best option.

At the core of it, respect your roommate, respect that their space is your space, and respect that they may just view the world a little differently. You don't have to be best friends with them. They will get on your nerves, make you upset, and maybe even snore. At the end of the day, they're just trying to survive college, too.

Nevertheless, your roommate situation is what you make it. If you want it to be miserable, it will become miserable. If you want it to be good, you'll face problems head-on, with mutual respect, and overcome any obstacles. If you ever feel unsafe or simply uncomfortable, it is totally okay to switch roommates. It isn't the end of the world, and it shouldn't be taken personally. Maybe y'all just weren't a good match.

After my first year, I learned that life is easier when you live with people who are genuinely invested in you. It was comforting to know that I would come home to people who wanted to help me in any way that they could. All of my best friends and I had strategically planned to live together our junior and senior year. We were all 18 when we planned it and seeing it come to reality made me realize that making friends with the people who lived across the hall from me was the best investment I've ever made.

Get to know your neighbors too

S: Whether you live in a hall-style dorm, suite-style, apartment, or house, it always pays off to meet your neighbors. My first-year neighbors have undoubtedly become some of my best friends in college. We grew up together at school. I partly believe that we all became friends because I began banging on everyone's door within the first week of school begging them to join my flag-football team (we went on to be 3-time champions).

Our Two Cents

➤ Consider rooming with someone you don't know for a brand new experience!

➤ Respect your roommate's belongings. No matter what kind of dorm, apartment, or house you live in, always respect someone else's personal property.

➤ If you're going to stay up late, make sure that you are not affecting your roommates' sleeping patterns.

➤ Nobody wants to live with someone they can't stand.

➤ Get to know your roommate and new neighbors. Visit their hometowns, or go on trips together. Do whatever it takes to see them for the people they are.

CHAPTER 6

The First Day of Class

*"Get excited, I wanted to jump
out of my seat!"*

A: You'll be more excited than you've ever been for the first day of class (**FDOC**). You'll wake up earlier than you need to, and you will probably get lost. Unless, you're a nerd like me and go and scope out the exact path you're going to take for each class.

S: I'd have to say that each **FDOC** of each year is totally different. Your first year, it's full of excitement as Austin mentioned. Your second year, the excitement wears off, but you're still just as eager. My third year was filled with confusion as I realized that I didn't know what I wanted to do with my life. Finally, senior year was so bittersweet.

My **FDOC** was pretty funny and I still blame my brother for some of the heartache…

I was in Europe the summer I was supposed to register for classes, so I let my brother make my schedule.

Looking back, it was very nice of him to do so (shout-out Kyle!) However, I am a big morning person, and I didn't have class until 11am every day. I remember waking up the first day and getting breakfast at the dining hall, walking to the bookstore and getting my books (rookie mistake**) and showing up to my first class 30 minutes early… you could say I was a bit excited.

The class was History 142, titled "Europe before 1450." That may not sound exciting to some of you, but I was almost jumping out of my seat by the time the class had started. I sat down at a round table and began introducing myself and talking to the other excited-looking first year students. I even had a 62-year-old man, who was in fact a student, sit across from me and strike up a conversation. I quickly realized that everyone in college is going through their own unique experience. I came to school fresh out of high school, but that may not be the path that everyone took. It was awesome to be able to learn about the new perspectives that can be taken from "non-traditional" students. My first class, which was supposed to last an hour and a half, was over within 29 minutes. Following my classes that day, I remember calling my mom and saying, "It wasn't exactly what I thought it was going to be." I thought my classes would ease into material. Instead, my professor said come to our next class having read 150 pages of material and be prepared to have a discussion, participation matters. After the first day, it was game-on from there on out.

A: One thing that I can't emphasize enough is the act of going to shake a professor's hand on the first day of class. For me, it was a way to get out of my comfort zone and to let the professor know who I was. This assertive act of going out of your way to meet your professor, especially in a large lecture class, will pay dividends in your comfort level in the classroom. If you're unsure of how to approach your professor just say, "Hi my name is (insert your name) and I wanted to tell you how excited I am to take your class!" Trust me, this might be hard at first, but it gets easier and easier every time. Also, professors love meeting students!

Be sure to jump out of your comfort zone every chance you can, even if it is on the first day of class.

Our Two Cents

➤ Walk your class schedule before the first day.

➤ Don't be late!

➤ Don't buy your books just yet- wait until you find out the required material and you might end up dropping the class.

➤ Before or after class, go and introduce yourself to your professors. First impressions mean everything!

➤ Make friends in your classes, no matter how old they are.

➤ Get excited on your first day (and stay excited), no matter how boring the topic may seem.

**Buying your books before the first day of class may seem like a great idea. After all, you want to be prepared for whatever the professor may throw at you. However, often times professors haven't updated their syllabus or have scanned a PDF version for you! A large portion of professors at my school signed an affordability pledge. They committed to keeping textbook costs under $50! Therefore, often times when I went to class, my professors would say not to worry about a specific book because they already had all the materials for us. I always found it helpful to wait until after I had the class to go buy the books. Plus, textbooks are HEAVY! There's simply no need to carry around a 75 pound book bag on your very first day.

CHAPTER 7

Choosing a Major

"Bring your passion with you!"

A: "What's your major? Why do you want to major in that? What are you going to do with that major?" When you get to college, you'll get bombarded with these questions everywhere you go. Choosing a major can be a hard task for some, and although it's a key component for graduation, your major doesn't always affect "what you want to do in life."

Before going to college, I knew that I wanted to be a business major, and I might be one of the rare few that never changed my major or even considered changing my major. However, I realize that some students enter college not having any idea what they want their major to be, and I am here to tell you THAT IS COMPLETELY FINE! Sometimes not knowing what you want your major to be can prove to be beneficial. It gives you an opportunity to explore subjects and find your calling.

S: I also came into college knowing what I wanted to study. However, halfway through my sophomore year, I took a communication intensive course. I really enjoyed learning about how people interpret information, how people make meanings, and what is important to humans on an individual and societal basis. Therefore, I added a second major!

A major is your intended area of study. Your school will have major requirements that make you take specific classes to fulfill your degree requirements. For example, I majored in Political Science, which meant I had to take a class called POLI 150: International Relations and Global Politics. I never thought I could come in and study anything outside of political science but it turned out that my interest was sparked in another area. Since I added a second major, that meant I had more degree requirements to receive my diploma. It doesn't matter if you have one or three majors, it is about pursuing what you are interested in. Since I became interested in studying how people interact with each other, I thought it would make sense to make it official.

Wondering how to choose major?
Wait no more!

Finding your passion: If you are unsure what you're passionate about, refer back to your goal list. Your goal list can open your eyes to what you really value in life. Passion can also be found by trying new things, which could include taking different types of classes, getting involved with different clubs on campus, or anything that gets you out of your dorm room meeting and interacting with new people.

If you can't determine what you're passionate about, follow the advice from Mike Rowe (the famous TV host), "Bring your passion with you!" In all things you do, whether it's homework, a first interview, or cheering on your university's team, be a passionate person.

Take different classes: General education requirements help students explore differing majors. These classes could consist of math classes, logical thinking classes, literary intensive courses, etc. – they'll vary depending on your school. Taking various classes allows you to explore different ideas and you may just end up enjoying something you never thought of before!

Meet with your academic advisor: Every college campus has an academic advising office. **PLEASE TAKE ADVANTAGE OF THIS!** I believe this is one of the most underutilized resources on every college campus. College academic advisors are there to help push you in the right direction with an unbiased point of view. They're also very passionate about helping college students and want to see you succeed.

Academic advisors can show you potential careers that may fit with each major, and they can also recommend the best class scheduling. Since all schools are different, it's impossible for me to recommend what the best classes are for you or when you should take them. Reaching out to your advisor will help you answer some of these questions.

Work hard, show up, and participate: Hard work beats talent—isn't that how the saying goes? That simple statement holds true in college. If you work hard in your classes, show up, and participate, you will reap the benefits. If you choose a major, and never show up for the classes, how will you know if that's the major you should be choosing?

After choosing a major, it is crucial to plan out what classes you are going to take to get you to graduation. Graduation comes faster than you think, and you want to make sure you are ready on the academic side of things first.

How to academically graduate in four years

Take at least fifteen hours per semester, unless you come in with credit: In order to graduate from most colleges, you need 120 credits/hours, meaning you'll need thirty credits per year or fifteen per semester. Most classes are three credits, and it is very doable to take fifteen credits per semester. Some students come in with AP, community college, or IB credit, though, which allows them to take less hours. These high school credits vary from college to college, and I advise checking with the admissions office of your school to see what will transfer as acceptable credit.

Summer School/Overloading/Underloading: Depending on your major, if you want to double major, or your academic workload, you might have to take summer school classes, or overload. Summer school classes are just shortened versions of regular classes in the summertime and can oftentimes be easier because you usually only take one or two classes in a smaller, more intimate setting.

On the flip side of that, during your senior year, you might have the opportunity to underload. I had the opportunity to take 7.5 hours during my last semester, and let me tell you, it was marvelous. In a later chapter I will talk about my social life, and that wouldn't have been possible without my hard work during the early stages of my college career.

Don't blink: Four years seems like a long time, but it will truly fly by, and before you know it you will be a senior. Try to enjoy each class you take, no matter how boring they may seem.

Choosing your major can seem like a daunting task, and for some it might seem harder to choose a major than they realized. However, I know you will make the right decision if you base it on your passion. I promise you won't be disappointed!

Our Two Cents

➤ Get ahead early, don't wait until your senior year to cram classes!

➤ "Bring your passion with you," no matter what you're doing.

➤ Get to know your academic advisor, they're an incredible resource that is underutilized.

➤ A major doesn't define your career path.

CHAPTER 8

College Classes

"Don't freak, you can pass the class."

A: News flash! You go to college to go to class, and going to class means there's exams, studying, and grades. Wooohooo! I know that gets you very excited… well, maybe not too excited, but you must learn that in order to be a successful college student, each of these aspects will need to be mastered or at least understood to make it through college.

S: Classes in college require a different set of skills. It is not about repeating information anymore. It is about a complex and deep understanding of course content and material. In some classes you may only have one grade, in another, you may have a quiz everyday. It is important to realize that grades do not make or break your college experience. You will be able to graduate, get a job, and ultimately succeed whether you make straight A's or not.

Exams

I have never tested well. Even in 3rd grade, multiple-choice test were not easy for me. With that being said, on my first final ever in college, I made a horrible grade. The class was U.S Government and Politics. I was devastated. This is my area of expertise; how could I make a low grade on something I understand so thoroughly and to which I plan to dedicate my life?

Making that low of a grade on my first final was a huge learning experience. I had to adjust everything that I knew about testing to accommodate a more rigorous academic curriculum. I had to read slower and understand deeper.

I came from a small public high school where I was challenged academically, but when I came to college the academic challenges I faced were at a different level. I eventually became a better test-taker and understood how to study for different types of classes. Believe it or not, studying for a history class and studying for Spanish require two vastly different studying styles. Therefore, I've got some tips on how and when to start studying for exams.

Studying

S: The day before is NOT the right time to start studying. Plan to study 4 to 5 days out. This allows you to not be stressed or pushed for time; you can spend the first few days reviewing material and the last two recalling information by mimicking a test.

The night before the test, go to bed early! The all-nighter is never worth it. Getting rest is so important so that you are alert and awake during the exam (coffee helps too). On test day, eat breakfast. You don't want to take your test on an empty stomach. Being hungry is all consuming and will be only thing you can think about when you're attempting to focus on your test. However, one of my favorite pieces of advice is simply to treat it like any other normal day.. There is no reason to stress yourself out. Make sure you have studied and be confident walking into the test.

Study groups can be helpful, especially if you all are able to quiz each other so that you all get the same amount of benefit out of the group. Beware of the study groups that turn into a catch-up session for people who skip class; if your study group turns into that, you're not getting what you could out of it! Sometimes, it's better to just study on your own.

Keep in mind that you can over-study. It is important to plan ahead and to take a few days to understand the material before either cramming the night before or studying three weeks in advance.

Grades and Classes

A: When I graduated high school, I had never received a B in any class. College changed that. College grades are different- yes, they matter, yes C's can get degrees, and depending on the class, yes, you can fail a class if you fail one exam, but it's not likely.

However, I would challenge you to look past what grades you get in a class and focus more on what you get out of each class.

S: You won't be the perfect student. You aren't supposed to be.

The class I learned the most from required me to be very uncomfortable. The class was called Introduction to Performance Studies. To be honest, I had no idea what performance studies was, and I still barely know. The class demanded that I perform skits, poems, and songs in front of my class, a group that at one point were total strangers. The very first day I had to perform a self-written slam poem. I called my poem, "How to be an Optimist," and it was really, really bad. However, the professor noticed that I tried. I put in a lot of effort; I had been to her office hours at the beginning of the week and attempted to perfect my poem. I ended up getting an A in the course, and it offered me the ability to use an open mind when approaching social situations. It was a positive experience for me because I am able to translate the skills I used (public speaking, empathic approaches to understanding), in my practical life. I invested in it, I learned from it, and I came out on the other side with a deeper understanding of how art impacts the world and ended up getting an A!

A: If you want to be a doctor, it means you've got to go to medical school. If you want to go to a prestigious med school, you better have prestigious grades. Yet, there are folks who have spotless GPAs and never get into their dream school. College isn't all about the grades; instead it's about what you get out of each class, how you can take that class, and how you make an impact on campus. Place some of your focus on studying, understanding the material and performing well on exams, but your focus shouldn't end with a letter grade.

Our Two Cents

➤ Strive to do your best, but don't get yourself down if you don't get the grade you wanted. Just work harder next semester.

➤ GPAs matter to some extent, but your experience matters more.

➤ If you get a bad grade and you don't like it, you better have listened to Savannah and went to office hours before you made that grade.

➤ Go to class!

CHAPTER 9

Professors

"Gateways for opportunities"

A: If you're like Savannah and me, we were close with our teachers all throughout grade school. Heck, both of our parents were educators. So, it might not come to your surprise that we both enjoyed writing this chapter of the book. To me, professors, the great ones, will challenge you — all very differently; they will get to know you on a personal level, if you let them, and they will prepare you for "The Real World" — some will even introduce you to job opportunities.

Each professor is different

Great professors can make the most boring topics the most interesting thing in the world. On the other hand, bad professors can make interesting topics very boring.
S: You'll find that you will become accustomed to a specific style of teaching. I prefer teachers who are interactive

and have open dialogues in class. I often found myself daydreaming in big lectures. Quickly, I figured out what my learning style and then adapted my course selection to professors who I knew were engaging to me.

Get to know your professors

Personal relationships with professors are important. The best way to get to know a professor is to go to their office hours. Go introduce yourself, ask for help on the first assignment to make sure that you have a clear understanding of what is expected. If you don't understand something in class, go to office hours. If you don't know why you made a certain grade, go to office hours. Always be respectful and kind, as it goes a long way to create a relationship with your professors! Don't show up on the last day of class asking for your grade to be raised if you have never been to office hours!

A: I am now three years out of college and still have some of my old professors on speed dial. The relationships you build with your professors in college don't have to end when you graduate. You truly never know what going to office hours or introducing yourself to a professor can do for your future. In my opinion, professors are one of the most underutilized resource on a college campus. No excuses- get to know your professors before it's too late.

Professors can introduce you to opportunities

S: Professors are gateways for opportunity. They are always looking to take on new projects and are always being asked to share information about jobs or internships. The professors that I engaged with loved to mentor. I actually had a professor offer me a job after a class one day. I was engaged and active during the class period and the professor asked if I would be willing to help her research women in politics in North Carolina. I agreed happily and was so thankful that I had established a relationship with this professor; she even just wrote my letters of recommendation for law school!

Professors rock so be engaging and make them your friends!

Let's make this simple: I've had good professors and bad professors. I once had a professor give me an 80% in participation because I was "too active" in class yet as I just told you, one offered me a job. However, professors exist here to connect you to the world, challenge your traditional ways of thinking, and ultimately make you talk about the course concepts outside of class. A great professor will learn with you, be patient, have clear expectations, and always be respectful.

Teaching styles vary dramatically between each class. The internet is full of professor information- websites like **ratemyprofessor.com** can be very helpful resources for general education requirements but also miss the mark often. The only people that fill out those ratings are people who feel very strongly, either good or bad. While these ratings can be helpful, they don't make or break the way one person teaches.

Our two cents

➤ Introduce yourself.

➤ Keep in contact throughout the semester.

➤ Be respectful of their time and teaching style.

➤ Invite them to lunch.

➤ Take advantage of their office hours.

➤ Keep in touch. It is important to maintain relationships with your professors following the semester you take their class. If you truly found a connection with the professor, make sure you continue meeting with them, and using them as a resource.

CHAPTER 10

Studying & Traveling Abroad

"Just go!"

S: Studying abroad may seem like an impossible task. I've heard things like: "it's too much money, I don't want to be too far from home" or folks are worried about going to a completely different place that they're not used to. Whatever the excuse might be, trust me- no excuse is valid. Studying abroad is incredible, and it is absolutely worth it.

I studied abroad in Copenhagen, Denmark for two months in between my sophomore and junior year. I went in the summer by myself. I didn't know anyone on the trip, I had two random roommates, and I flew across the world with nothing but a backpack.

I ended up meeting some very wonderful people. I made global friends, and friends from all across the United States. I have kept up with these friends throughout the rest of college and still consider them to be some of my closest confidants. While I learned so much about a culture far different from my own, I also was able to develop social skills, and very important life skills. Adapting to a place much different than your own allows you to view the world in a more holistic perspective.

Student's often think that classes aboard are easy and boring. However, the classes I took challenged me to think differently. For example, I took a course called Espionage in the Cold War. Due to the geographic location of Copenhagen, I was able to learn about the Cold War from an entirely different perspective and understand how central Copenhagen was to the United States during this period. I also took a class called Cross-Cultural Communications that included a week-long study tour to Northern Ireland to study the Catholic-Protestant Conflict. It was incredibly helpful to actually go out into the world and learn through experience rather than reading from a textbook.

The coolest part about studying abroad for me was to apply the things I had learned in the classroom to the real world. I intentionally visited places I had read about before and was able to get a deeper understanding of what I was studying. The whole point of going abroad is to learn in a different way; if you aren't invested in understanding things with a new perspective, you won't get as much out of the experience. Invest yourself in the community around you to get the full experience.

Sometimes study abroad really pushes you!

A: Studying abroad requires some sacrifice. For me, I had to take a student loan in order to pay for my two-week trip to South Africa. For others who go during the school year, they miss out on events on campus. Like Savannah said, there's no excuse: it is very worth it to miss events on your campus to study abroad, and the most important part of studying abroad, is it makes you jump out of your comfort zone. It just happened to be that my jump included swimming with Great White Sharks! **

I feel like I tell students to "jump out of their comfort zone" a million times during my presentations. Studying abroad is just one piece of jumping out of your comfort zone, but in my opinion, it's one of the most fun and rewarding.

Traveling aboard opens your eyes

When I graduated from high school, I didn't have a passport. I had only traveled to Myrtle Beach, SC and Pigeon Forge, TN- that really shows the country boy in me! When I got to college, my eyes were opened to people from different places, backgrounds, and experiences. The people I got to meet motivated me to travel, and after you travel once, you can't stop- it's like a drug!

Since college graduation, I have had the opportunity to travel to 8 more countries, which introduced me to more beautiful people, created friendships that'll last a lifetime, and encouraged me to keep traveling.

When you take the initial jump out of your comfort zone to travel, it's scary, exciting, and sometimes it takes a hit to your bank account. Yet, it's so worth it. Never make excuses for travel, because you never know who's out there. Just go!

Our two cents

- ➤ Stop thinking about the money, because it's worth it! If you can figure out a way to make it happen, do it.
- ➤ Find a place where you can explore your passion and apply to that program.
- ➤ Go meet with a study abroad advisor to understand your schools' programs in more detail. Most schools offer scholarships for the different programs, you just have to apply!
- ➤ Begin planning your trip after your first semester in college!

**In case you didn't know, South Africa is home to "shark alley." Every year Discovery Channel films great white sharks at "shark alley" for their features on Shark Week. When Discovery Channel isn't there filming, they let tourists like my classmates and me get into a cage surrounded by water, right where those big sharks swim.

As the boat made its way from the shore, I began to get more and more nervous. Then the eight-person cage was dropped into the water, and the "chum man" started chumming. Within minutes, a large gray object darted by, probably nine feet long, a "small one," the guides said.

Being the impatient one, I wanted to be one of the first

in the water. I nervously pulled on the wetsuit, strapped on a GoPro camera, and hopped into the water.

"Left, down, down, down," the guide yelled as great whites darted by the cage. I remember coming up out of the water yelling in excitement. This was the coolest thing I had ever done. During some parts of the dive, I thought I was watching a video, it seemed so unreal. Then, all of a sudden, this huge object appeared from my right side. "Was that Megalodon?" I screamed at the guide.

CHAPTER 11

Involvement on Campus

"Good news! Only 6 meetings tonight!"

S: Getting involved will make or break your college experience. When I arrived at college I was over-eager to get involved. After all, I had juggled school, sports, clubs and just about everything else in high school. I was determined to "do it all" again in college. I very quickly learned that college is way different.

I dove head first into several different organizations the first semester of the first year. I joined Student Government, a PanHellenic sorority (Alpha Chi Omega), the dance marathon team, campus recreation, intramural teams, three political groups, amongst many other things. I quickly learned that I was in over my head. I had to prioritize school work. I ended up focusing on only a few of the clubs for my first year.

I found three organizations that were really impactful for me: one that was fun, one that was social, and one that was professional-oriented.

Fun

At 5:30am every Thursday morning I would climb out of my lofted twin bunk bed, put on my sneakers, and start my mile and a half run to a small building behind, what seemed to be, a giant dump truck. I taught yoga to the landscaper staff on campus.

It was undoubtedly one of the most rewarding and fun things that I did throughout my time at school. I became good friends with many of the workers. I got to know about their families and what they do for fun. It really shaped my college experience because I recognized that all of the people who work on campus are here to serve the students. It may not always feel like people are on the students' team but ultimately, they wouldn't be working for a university if they weren't.

Getting to know the landscaping staff also instilled in me to say extra thank-you's to the dinning staff and the house-keepers, a few with whom I got particularly close. Joining this organization allowed me to see the human in others. I learned that life truly is all about how you treat others.

Join an organization that makes you truly happy. Join something you genuinely enjoy. It will bring you new friends, new perspectives, and hopefully you'll learn something about life on the way.

Social

I joined a social organization as well. For me, that was my sorority. I rushed in my first semester of school, which was a stressful process. However, I ended up in the right place for me. The biggest benefit that I got out of it was meeting people who were like-minded. The girls were driven, excitable, and passionate about others. On my campus, sororities and fraternities often have housing, and it was awesome for me to be able to have a literal home away from home. I always felt welcome, included, and heard in my sorority. Some of my very best friends have been in the same organization with me throughout my four years.

While sororities can be controversial, it was important and upon reflection, necessary for me to join an organization where I could relax and be my goofy self without any repercussions. The sorority also held several service oriented events and supported other organizations across campus. We often helped out at women's shelters and raised thousands of dollars every year to help sustain community partners.

Joining a social organization allows you to immediately meet new people. A social organization doesn't have to be sorority or fraternity; it could be the mock trial team or the dance marathon team. Organizations are innately social, but being intentional about what you chose will be beneficial for you in the long run. Being able to maintain relationships with people outside of your immediate friend group is crucial to your college career, social organizations allow you to keep in touch with a variety of different people.

Professional

I joined Student Government because I am passionate about it. I have a desire to be involved in local government and politics and I thrive in situations where I am surrounded by people. My freshman year, I joined a first-year council and had the opportunity to plan events and create a community for my classmates. It allowed me to create an entirely separate network full of friends and colleagues. However, I quickly learned that there is a hierarchy within clubs and involvement opportunities. You have to work your way up to leadership positions. I was a bit disappointed that I wasn't able to dive right in and be a key contributor to the organization. It was necessary for me to work my way up the organization. I simply wasn't ready to tackle some of the broader university issues. I also didn't understand the complexities of some of the more difficult roles. In order to succeed in those roles, institutional knowledge was necessary, which is something you simply don't have your first semester in college. These years were transformative for me. I set out a long-term goal and was able to achieve it by working hard and focusing on the things that mattered to me. This was for the best. I didn't understand campus culture or the organization enough to be in a strong leadership position yet.

After my first year, I was then able to move up the ranks and gain leadership experience. Not all clubs or organizations are like this but don't be discouraged by the ones that are. Joining this organization gave me an end goal. I was motivated to be the leader of the organization and perused it throughout my time as a student. It was fun, impactful, and challenging work. It demanded my very best, at all times, and I had to be prepared to give it. This organization shaped my personal and professional life and I developed some very important interpersonal skills from being involved.

Professional organizations offer a lot of opportunities. They allow you to network or give you first access to internships. They allow you to develop your personal and professional skills that will translate into real life. Organizations like these are important because they help you learn about how to navigate different, or complicated, scenarios that will apply to your working life. Also, professional organizations demonstrate to employers that you are a serious candidate!

While these three clubs had a big impact on my life. I tried other organizations out that didn't have the same impact- that's absolutely okay! I learned what I did and didn't like by trying new things. An example for me would be a faith based group. I tried several faith groups upon coming to school. I never quite found one I was entirely comfortable in. However, I think faith can come alive in many different ways during a time of transition. Austin had a completely different experience; this is to say that what may be for one person, may not be for another.

Other involvement on campus

A: College is diverse; it's diverse in almost every way possible. College brings students together of all colors, all backgrounds, and from all faiths. With worshipers of different faiths coming together, there are times when students of differing beliefs might confront each other and/or learn something new about a faith that they didn't understand before.

Growing up a Christian, I went to church with my family, went to bible school every summer, and read the Bible on occasion. However, when I got to college, my parents were no longer there to make me go to church. There were way more distractions, and for the first time, I had to figure out what I truly believed. I can't speak to other students' faith experiences, but for some reason coming to college scared me because I thought I would lose my own faith.

College allowed me to really find out what I truly believed. It allowed me to get involved with Christian organizations on my own and go to church if I felt led to do so. I will not profess that I always stayed the course of what I believe; college challenged my faith every day. However, that's why I believe getting involved with faith-based organizations on campus really made my college experience so impactful. I was able to build relationships with people that believed the same thing as I did, and these people typically pushed me in the way that I needed. If I got off track or strayed from my values, these people were the first to tell me.

S: Clubs and organizations are great. However, you can also get involved in the campus community a variety of different ways, like attending campus events: art exhibits, sporting events, plays, etc.

When I went to school, I bought into the sports culture. I bought jerseys, face paint, crazy hair- anything that would demonstrate my support for the team and the school. I immediately felt welcome among my fellow classmates; we were all yelling at the ref that he had missed a call.

Sports create a sense of connection, an entire student body rallying behind one thing creates a sense of camaraderie like not other. The first home basketball game was one to remember. The city was buzzing with excitement because, finally, basketball season was back. On game day, everyone would drop all of their homework to tune into the game. Students would line up for hours, in sunshine, rain, or snow, outside of the stadium just to catch a glimpse of the players. Going to the first game of the year is when my school finally felt like home. I would encourage you to attend these events, even if you're not the biggest sports fan. You'll be surprised as to what you can find.

Overall, getting involved helps you meet people. My first year I joined organizations that ultimately gave me some of my best friends in college. Put yourself out there, join weird clubs, and if you're like me you'll be excited when you have six meetings in one night!

Our Two Cents

➤ Get involved early.

➤ Commit deeply to a minimal number of organizations.

➤ Attend different campus events! This allows you to make new friends and possibly get free food (which is always a win)!

➤ Don't be intimidated by something completely new - you never know who, what or where that organization may take you!

CHAPTER 12

Working in college

"We don't all win the lottery."

A: Unless you plan on winning the Mega Million Jackpot, you will most likely have to work in college. Working in college allows you to become more independent, thus better preparing you for the **real world**.

We all come from different backgrounds: some of us have no money, some of us have some money, and a small few have a lot of money. Whatever boat you're in, this advice still applies to you, no matter who is paying for your college experience.

I came from a family that could assist me in paying for college (I will actually finish paying off my student loans by the end of 2019, right after this book is published); however, I still needed to work during my four years in college.

Jobs in college can vary. Some of my jobs consisted of being a brand ambassador for startups, in which I would promote their products. For instance, I worked for

Insomnia Cookies and gave out free cookies to students on campus. I held other traditional jobs like working for the admissions office and the alumni center. So, whether you're handing out cookies, or using a scanner for 8 hours a day, treat each job with respect and the employers that come along with it!

If you're fortunate enough to have your parents pay for your entire college experience or you receive a full ride scholarship, I would still strongly advise you to find some type of work, whether for pay or volunteer. Working in college can teach you so much more than just having a few dollars extra to spend. If you're working to pay for college, know that you're the best kind of college student. You're making the most of every second because you're paying for it and you won't let anytime go to waste. Your hard work will pay off, trust me!

Savannah had a very similar experience to mine and benefited heavily from working a variety of jobs on campus:

S: I worked a variety of jobs during my college career. It was important for me to be able to provide things for myself. I worked at campus recreation, babysat, held an undergraduate research position, and my senior year I worked about forty hours a week on campus.

In my role as the Student Body President, my campus demanded every ounce of my attention. However, I made less than two dollars an hour for my work. Therefore, I had to take every opportunity I could to make a buck. I ended up taking a 3-hour test for the psychology department to study and even picked up trash for the city to make money. Again, it was important to me to be as financially independent as I could. However, working during my time at school opened my eyes to the importance of a college education. With my degree I was guaranteed to make more than 2 dollars an hour and was certain I wouldn't be taking any more tests. Working made me realize that school is an investment in your livelihood, not just a chore or another box you have to check.

Working in college can be frustrating...

Or at least it was for me. When I got to college I was so ready to begin earning real money. I would get paychecks that ranged from $3.00 to $300 at very weird times during the month. It is safe to say that my income was not sustainable. I tried very hard to budget and to save but it became increasingly difficult the older I became. I spent over half of my income on food and 8 dollar beers. However, I also spent money on going with friends to the movies, to arcades, or spontaneous weekend trips. My senior year, I spent over five hundred dollars on graduate school applications. If you don't budget for your future, you will be in serious trouble.

Now, while I firmly believe working is very important, it is also necessary to take a break. I found myself going to class from 9am-4pm and working from 5-10pm some days and I was exhausted. I intentionally blocked off "play" time, where I would simply put away all home-work and just hang out with friends. My advice to you, if you're willing and able, get a side job. It will teach you time management skills, financial agency, and you will be able to meet an entirely different group of people.

Our two cents

➤ Find a small job after you have time to settle into college.

➤ Prioritize school over your job.

➤ When you accept your first job, be sure and manage your time effectively. Some jobs can take up a decent amount of time, and you'll want to stay balanced.

➤ When your first paycheck rolls in, be sure to manage your money wisely. Don't go crazy!

CHAPTER 13

Taking care of you

"I showered twice today. #SelfCare"

S: Being healthy is a holistic goal. You can't be healthy if you're only partially taking care of yourself. It is very easy to put your health on the back-burner when you are in college. No one is around to tell you to eat fruits and vegetables. You have to do these things on your own. Other things take priority and you simply may forget to eat a meal or won't leave enough time to sleep. However, it is incredibly important to get into a routine that allows you to sleep, eat, exercise, and relax.

Prioritize sleep

You will need it to get through the day and to be the best student. My first semester I was staying up until 3am for literally no reason. I caught myself being drowsy and not as attentive in class. I then put myself on a sleep schedule during the week. I went to bed around 11pm and got up at 7am This schedule allowed me to structure my day, while still having fun with all my friends. Of course, this schedule was broken every weekend, I stayed rested during the week!

Eat a balanced diet, not just pizza

The dining hall can be your best friend or your worst enemy. The tables are overcrowded, and the food is a hit or miss. However, the cafeterias are littered with healthy options. You'll be able to try new foods and chose what you put in your body. Whatever you like eating and whatever you chose to eat, make sure to find some sort of balance.

Get into an exercise routine

That can be as simple as walking to class or even going to the gym. I kept up with an exercise routine by playing intramural sports. I played soccer, basketball, flag football, softball, street hockey, and every other intramural that was offered. It was a great way for me to have fun in a competitive way that kept me healthy. Having an exercise buddy is a great way to hold yourself accountable and to make sure that you are consistently exercising.

Have fun!

Whether that is reading a good book or watching television it is so important to unwind. School is stressful and can be overwhelming, you will need to find an activity that allows you to balance all of the craziness.

A: Right when I graduated high school my cousin gave me this piece of advice, "College is all about the choices you make, Austin. The choices." He winked at me, laughed, but then said "seriously."

I didn't fully understand his advice until I graduated college, but it still rings true today. In college, you'll most likely have more freedom than you've ever had. You'll have the freedom to go to sleep when you want to, eat what you want to whenever you want to, workout, and most importantly, hang out with whomever you want to. Freedom in college is a beautiful thing, yet for some, it can be scary.

The simple choices you make do make a big difference. So have the time of your life, but be smart in your choices. Going to bed early the night before a big exam is probably the right move versus going to a party down the hall. It's the little things that add up in college that eventually turn into big things.

Our Two Cents

➤ If you're not getting enough sleep, create a sleep schedule.
➤ Try new foods, maintain a balanced diet, and don't eat too many cookies in the dining hall.
➤ Be creative with your social choices. Choose throwing frisbee in the quad, a hike, a pickup

basketball game, or tennis, even if you've never played, that's part of the fun!

➤ College is all about choices. You can choose to eat pizza or a salad, you can choose to sleep or to party, but make sure you're making the right choices for you and those goals that'll be hanging up on your wall!

CHAPTER 14

Service

"It's about people."

A: While in college, stay grounded.

College isn't meant to make you selfish, but it makes you very independent. When you arrive on your college campus, you'll be so caught up in your class schedule, meeting new people, and getting involved in clubs and organizations. All of the opportunities on a college campus make it very easy to only focus on yourself. However, if you seek to do so, college can also make serving people an enjoyable, enriching activity.

Savannah's entire college career is the embodiment of what it means to serve on a college campus, and something that every college student should strive for!

S: I have always had a passion to serve. I joined an organization called Buckley Public Service Scholars upon coming to school. The program required that I hit benchmark goals of service throughout my four years at school. At the beginning of the program, they ask you to define your personal philosophy of service. I quickly wrote mine down and it still guides my decision making to this day. Before committing myself to something I ask myself a series of questions:

Who am I serving?
What tangible impact will this make?
When will the outcome be noticeable?
How does this affect the lives of those around me?

Throughout my service work I quickly found that sometimes, there is a comfort to be found in strangers; people are willing to tell their deepest secrets to those they've met only minutes before. Desperate for help, and already dealing with judgment from those they don't know, they plead for someone to listen as they confess to mistakes made long ago. I witnessed this phenomenon repeatedly during my work with Legal Aid of North Carolina. I was working as a navigator for the Affordable Care Act under Legal Aid in Durham, North Carolina. My job was to meet with prospective clients and determine whether or not they were eligible to receive healthcare coverage. I worked many hours with people I had never seen before, but I left knowing their life stories.

Through clubs and organizations, internships and jobs, I found myself realizing one fundamental truth: service is about people. It isn't a title or a resume booster, it certainty isn't a headline thanking you for all you've done, but it is about creating lasting, sustainable impact. That impact can be as little as making someone feel welcome to creating a long-term project that will affect generations of students to come.

Being able to give back to the community that helped build you is a fundamental pillar of any university. It is necessary to recognize that without philanthropy, many of the things you hold dear may not even exist.

A: As you read in an earlier chapter, in order to be a successful college student, you have to learn how to manage your time wisely. Managing your time also means finding quality in your time, and not just quantity. If you're very involved on your college campus, and its only activities that are going to make you excel, take a step back. College isn't all about you, it's about the people you get to impact along the way and that will impact you.

Our Two Cents

➤ Search for service-oriented clubs/organizations on your college's website. Most universities have a list of all clubs/organizations. If you know the area that you are passionate about, check out some related organizations.

➤ Talk to friends, older students, or professors. Your best resource on your college campus is the people. Talk to others, see what's offered and what they would recommend. You never know the opportunities that can spawn from conversation!

➤ Get out of your comfort zone. In my last stretch of college (second semester senior year), I (Austin) volunteered to be an auctioneer at a charity auction for an organization raising money for a summer camp! I had never had an experience like this before and it was really cool to help make an impact!

CHAPTER 15

Dating & Friendships

"There's such a thing as a bad date"

S: This chapter isn't a tell-all of the best and worst dates I've ever had. It's a chapter about dating advice and simply things I learned while meeting new people and enjoying the company of others.

Dating in college

There are several different types of *dating* in college. There's 'I've only got eyes for you' dating, 'we aren't together but I would get mad if they went out with someone else' dating, and then there's 'I'm really not sure, we will figure it out later' dating. Dating could mean going to get coffee and never talking again. It could mean going on a cocktail date, or it could mean a movie, or going to watch a sporting event. Whatever it may be, I think it is important to date in college so that you know the type of person you may want to marry or not marry one day. Dating is your own prerogative. If you want to date someone different every weekend, do it. If you don't want to date at all, don't. Dating is a personal choice.

My first year at school I intentionally did not get involved with anyone. I simply didn't want a boyfriend and decided it I would be best for me to ground myself first. I needed to find my college friends, figure out how to navigate campus, and focus on school before I did anything else.

During my college experience, I dated someone for over a year. We had so much fun. Looking back on it now, we were just kids. No one knows what they're doing but I'm happy we got to figure some of this craziness out together. After that, I went to dinner with a few different people here and there, had a few coffee dates, went to a couple of cocktails but nothing really ever came out of it. The timing wasn't right for me and I decided I needed to focus on my future and friends.

Dating in college is... an experience

I now know that I hate spicy food, you can steam zucchini in the microwave, and that a boy that doesn't clean his bathroom, certainly isn't the boy for me. But I also know that it is important for me to date someone who works hard, loves sports, and calls his mom.

Whoever says, "there's no such thing as a bad date" is absolutely wrong. I once had someone pick me up, blaring hip-hop so loudly we couldn't talk in the car. We went to a food truck, notorious for being terrible, and no surprise it was. My date only talked about two things, professional soccer and himself. I was only interested in one of those topics. From this experience, I learned that no one in their 20s knows what to do. Everyone has a different idea of what they want.

I firmly believe that the world works in funny ways and if it is meant to be then life will always bring you back together. That may be the next month or it may be in 30 years but if it is meant to be, it will be.

Friendships in college

One of my favorite times in college was when everyone returns from winter or summer breaks. Everyone is excited to see each other. While the "welcome back" week is usually filled with events and parties, I've learned that friendship isn't all about the "Oh wow!" moments. It's a culmination of the little things. One of my favorite memories is returning to school, grabbing a burger and sharing a side of fries with my buddies, catching up, and reaffirming why I love these people so much.

I am surrounded by people who have the same mentality of life that I do. We work very hard and we play a little harder. My friends are always achieving big things, whether that is getting a full time job, getting into graduate schools, or pursuing prestigious internships, these people are go-getters. They consistently push me to give my very best. I surrounded myself with these types of people because they drive me to do better.

There have been times when people who I thought were my friends *threw me under the bus*, and that feeling sucks. I quickly realized though that I didn't have to be friends with anyone who wasn't rooting for me. Obviously, I am still cordial and respectful to these people, offering smiles and hellos as we pass on the street, but I refuse to surround myself with people with whom I don't share a mutual investment. I've made good friends. I've made bad friends. I've been a good friend, and at times, a bad one. Through these experiences, I learned that friendship isn't transactional.

My friends have made me a more holistic person. When I came to school, I didn't know everything about the world. I didn't realize how people operated so differently. I was stuck in my small town head and believed that there was only one right way to do something. My friends were able to expand my worldview and make me more empathic. I encourage you to find the people that make you a better person.

In high school, I was friends with some people due to proximity. College is different because in order to maintain a relationship, you must actively pursue your friends. You'll learn that you have to make time for your friends because everyone has a busy schedule. Do your best to keep up with those you care about. Things can always get in the way or timing may not work out, but I've learned that just checking in on those you care about has a meaningful impact.

Again, you'll meet some of the most amazing people while you're in school. These people will go on to be your biggest cheerleaders and best friends for your entire life. Everyone you meet in college will help you evolve into the person you want to be. There may be friends that you never talk to again, and that's okay. Not everyone is meant to be in your life forever. Find people that make you better and stick with them.

Our Two Cents

➤ If your mom doesn't like them, you shouldn't either.

➤ You're still young. Don't get fixated on one person.

➤ Apologize. It's never too late to ask someone for forgiveness.

➤ Respect others. Relationships are a two-way street. Treat the other person with complete respect.

➤ Your college friends let you sleep on their couches when they get into the 'real world,' and I've crashed on many couches! Always stay connected to the people you meet in college. If they were worth your time then, then make them worth it **after** college.

CHAPTER 16

Social media

"So I looked at her brother's girlfriend's sister's Instagram..."

A: Social media in college is huge. It can be a helpful tool: you can find information faster than ever, you can connect with someone instantly, and it can even help you build a 'brand.' However, social media can also cause anxiety, depression, and most importantly, it draws you away from the present. Doesn't it just bother you when you're talking to someone and they're scrolling through Instagram?

In today's time, everything you do is recorded. That keg stand? Someone snapped it, it's on someone's story, or someone for sure has it saved on their iCloud account. If you're going to say or do something, and there is a slight chance it can be on social media, be sure you're not afraid of the consequences. Now, I know what you might be thinking, "No way this will happen to me, I know all of my friends and they wouldn't do that..."

During my time in college, social media wasn't as prevalent as it is today. Yet, it still had a major impact on my classmates' future. There was a student a few years older than me that had a full-time job taken away because of an inappropriate picture that was shared on Twitter. Recruiting teams (for full time jobs) now check your social media outlets as much as they check your resume.

S: There is a time and a place for social media. That time and place is not when you're eating dinner with your friends or in class. However, it took me a bit to learn this lesson. I was in a Greek Mythology class and my professor decided to have an "exit quiz." He tested us on the material we learned that day. I was so caught up in snapchat and Instagram to even pay attention in class. Needless to say, I failed that quiz.

My first year, I was so connected to social media. It was the best way for me to stay in touch with all of my newfound friends. We snapchatted, followed each other on Twitter, and became friends on Facebook, all in the same day. However, these "followers' are meaningless until you get to know the person behind the screen. Put down the phone and engage in real conversations. You'll be surprised what you can find out about a person when you talk to them face to face.

Part of me is still learning the lesson of being disconnected. I'm learning about the addictive habits social media can have. I'm learning about the negative affects of creating preconceived notions about people I've never met. I'm learning how what you post as a teenager can haunt you in your future. I'm learning that I feel like a better person, am genuinely happier, and feel more present when I am off my phone. It may take awhile for you to get there, but the older you become the more you value real relationships, rather than artificial ones.

However, I still post pictures and comment on friends' posts. I retweet awesome sports moments but my social media has cleaned up to be more professional as I enter the working world. I wish I would've had this same advice before coming to school. No one could predict the intrusive nature of social media back then, but we can now. My advice to you is to never post anything your grandma wouldn't like. I'll leave it at that.

Social media can be a positive tool

A: Even though social media can be a dangerous tool, it can also be very impactful. I had many friends who built a **brand** for themselves. These brands allowed them to have thousands of followers, make extra money, and eventually score a job that allowed them to pursue their passion. Building a brand isn't the only positive thing that can come from social media, for myself, it was a way to share with my family and other friends what I was doing, and a way that I could keep tabs on them as well. It allowed me to see where my friends were traveling, which motivated me to want to go there, and lean on them for tips and advice of where to go and what to see.

Social media is great in moderation. There's an old saying in the south that goes like this: "Don't overstay your welcome." The saying should be applied to social media. Stay for a little bit, but don't park your eyes there for more than 5-10 minutes at a time. You've got college to live and experience, but it can't be done through other people's posts. Go live your best life, so you can post your own experiences!

Our two cents

➤ Limit your time on your device. iPhones allow you to set restrictions on app usage, so take advantage of that!

➤ If you're with your friends, keep your phone in your pocket. Don't even put it on the table, it's a distraction.

➤ If you're going to put it on your story or Insta-gram, make sure it's something your future em-ployer would approve of, and remember that social media posts last a lifetime.

➤ There is a time and place for social media.

➤ When in class turn on the **Do Not Disturb** feature.

CHAPTER 17

Partying

"Yeah, I'm down for a beer...or six?"

S: "Goooooooooood morning, it's time to take shots!" That was a real sentence uttered to me at approximately 7:15am on the last day of class my first year. My college experience is filled with weird stories like this. However, I want to make two important distinctions before diving into this chapter: **1) You do not have to drink if you do not want to. 2) There is a safe way to party.**

My senior year, it was almost like a ritual. People would simply show up at my house around 9 or 10pm and we would play drinking games and enjoy each other's company every Thursday and Saturday night. Around 11:30 PM we would go off to our favorite bar, enjoy a drink with friends, and see where the night took us. Sometimes that would be to get some chili cheese fries, sometimes that would be straight home to bed. We enjoyed having drinks because it allowed us all to get together. It wasn't necessarily about having a beer, but more about being surrounded by the people you love.

I was at a bar once on game day. I entered a raffle and ended up winning 15 free cases of the always delicious, Natural Light (HAHA). I won around 300 free beers. It took me and my friends months to go through the cases. We played tons of beer pong on my front porch on nice days and even more card games when it was cold. There were countless laughs shared around a lukewarm Natty Light.

I want to make an important note. Partying in college is a **completely** different experience for girls than it is for boys. Ladies, you have to be conscious of other people. If your drink doesn't taste right, put it down. If you feel uncomfortable, tell someone. Don't walk home alone. I also don't always think guys recognize when they are making girls uncomfortable (or vice versa). It is okay to leave a conversation if it is weird. In my experience, these instances have been rare but they have happened. It is more important to be safe than to have a good time.

A: Savannah is exactly right, partying in college is completely different for girls than it is for boys. I would even say that partying is different for every single person. When I got to college, I didn't drink at all. In fact, my first sip of alcohol was when I was 19 in England (AND I was legal). I didn't really drink or party again until I turned 21. Even though I didn't party during my early college years, I still enjoyed my time and don't regret not partying until I was 21.

As a male, especially in today's time, you have to be safe in everything that you do. If you're drinking and another person is involved, especially sexually, things can get very complicated. When in doubt, or if you're too drunk to function, always walk away. It is never worth it to risk your future on a potential situation that could turn out very negatively.

The 'hookup' culture in college exists. If you decide to drink and partake in 'going home with another person' for a *hookup* (which can be defined very differently by different people), then I urge you to be safe. Use protection and remember **no means no!**

Partying as a male is much different and if you aren't careful it can be a very dangerous activity. Just be legal, respectful, and safe.

After the partying is over

S: Hangovers are real. They happen, they suck, but you still have to be functional. Laying in bed until 6pm because you are too hungover is probably an indicator that you overdid it. That shouldn't happen all that often. You should never miss a class, lunch with a friend, or an important meeting because you are too hungover.

With all that said, several of my friends in college simply didn't like to drink. They had just as much fun as the rest of us. Don't ever feel pressured to do something you truly do not want to do. I enjoyed 'partying' in college because there won't be another time in my life where

I can do such a thing. I enjoyed a good beer and making memories with my friends. If you want to drink, do so safely. If you don't, that's fine too.

Our Two Cents

➤ Stay with a buddy, being safe should be your number one priority.

➤ Order different drinks to see what you like, do you really want to be stuck drinking the same thing for the rest of your life?

➤ Don't use alcohol as an excuse for your reckless behavior. Being able to drink means that you are an adult, so act like one. Be responsible.

➤ Don't get peer pressured. If you do not want to go out, don't. You are in control of your decisions. Others may try to influence you, but their opinions simply do not matter.

➤ Never drive! Uber and Lyft are responsible ways of transportation.

CHAPTER 18

Preparing for life after college

"Be ready, it comes fast!"

A: I'm a big believer that college isn't the best four years of your life, but it's by far **the most unique four years of your life.** College is one of the only times that you are surrounded by young, ambitious students who are pursuing their dreams.

Don't let college be the best four years of your life, you must prepare for what's next. Preparing for what's next doesn't start during your senior year, or when you pick your major - preparing for what's next begins when you move in. I don't mean that you start applying for jobs when you start college, but the things you do while in college will impact the opportunities and the life you have post-graduation.

When I started writing the first version of this book, I didn't realize the activities I was involved with on campus would majorly affect my post-college life. My friends, professors, and the opportunities I took on campus all positioned me for the career and life that I have now as a 24-year-old.

In high school, I remember kids saying, "Oh, he's going to peak in high school, or if he doesn't, he's going to peak in college." That comment always stuck in the back of my head. For starters, it frustrated me. I knew college was going to be a wonderful, enriching time in my life, yet it wasn't going to define me. **So, no, I didn't peak in college, and you won't either**. We hope this book will give you the tools to make the most of the college journey, and better prepared for the next.

Some of the following chapters might not make as much sense to you if you're still in high school or just graduated. However, these are chapters that I would hold onto, and remember as you progress throughout your college experience.

The final chapters of the book are aimed to help you take advantage of your time on campus, so that you won't be freaking out come your senior year. Learning how to network effectively will help you score your first internship, which will eventually lead you to your first job. If you have aspirations of gaining a higher degree than undergraduate, Savannah will share with you her experience of applying to law school, which can relate to any post-graduate education selection. And, finally, if you've ever wondered what it's like to graduate college and tackle the real world, I'll give you a sneak peak.

Our Two Cents

➤ Four years in college go really fast, make the most of every second in college.

➤ Begin preparing for graduation the day you move-in.

➤ Your involvements on campus can greatly impact your post-college plans.

CHAPTER 19

Networking

"Don't forget your business cards!"

A: Opportunities on a college campus come in all shapes and sizes. Some of these opportunities come by signing up for an email list, some come by showing up, but most of the time, opportunities come from meeting the right people and networking effectively.

The word network means to connect and speak with others, such as students, professors, or potential employers, in order to exchange information like your email, phone number, or business card. Networking can be done in any setting: in the classroom, during an event, playing a sport, anywhere! People who are great networkers are always connected to what is going on around them.

I was one of those guys who loved his campus. I loved my campus so much that I became a tour guide, made a business card, and handed it out to anyone that would take it from me. In order to be an effective networker, especially in college, business cards help you stand out.

I'd recommend designing and purchasing business cards during your first or second year in college. They can be super affordable and purchased via Vistaprint.

Networking might not seem as important to you as a first-year college student; heck, maybe not even as a sophomore. However, networking to me isn't all about getting a job. It's about learning how to communicate with people, how to react in different situations, and how to maintain a relationship over a period of time. Whether you realize it or not, the day you move in to your dorm, you're 'networking.' When you begin to meet new friends in college, you're networking, and even when you meet your first professors. Be sure to leave a lasting impression, and if you desire, which I strongly encourage, create relationships that last your entire collegiate career and beyond. You never know how a relationship you make as a first year student can benefit you years down the road!

During my senior year, one of my professors gave me this advice: "It's not who you know; it's who knows you on a favorable basis." For instance, you want to be that kind of person that shows up positively in other people's conversations. Always be respectful while networking, and always look the other person in the eye. You never know if the person you are talking to could be the one to open the door to the next job or opportunity. Make the most of every person you interact with, no matter who they are.

Our Two Cents

➤ Networking is a two-way street. Learn to listen.

➤ Treat everyone as if they are the President of the United States. This is one of my favorite pieces of advice. No matter who the person is, no matter what, treat them with respect.

➤ Follow up after you meet. This is so crucial. After meeting someone for the first time, send a follow-up email, letter, call, or extend some kind of communication to thank them for their time and to learn more about their opportunity.

➤ Don't forget a handshake and a smile goes a long way.

➤ Business cards aren't just for business people.

CHAPTER 20

Internships

"This might lead to a job..."

S: Internships have the ability to impact your career placement out of college. It is important to have internship experience. It demonstrates to employers that you are passionate about a career, a hard worker, and that you are eager to learn about your field of interest.

I held several internships throughout college, all unpaid. That part sucked, but I gained valuable experience that I am able to touch on in interviews, networking opportunities, or even in the classroom.

I interned for United Way, Legal Aid, several local government offices, amongst other places. It was helpful for me because I got to see how the world functioned and where I would best fit. I learned that I am simply not meant for the courtroom, but that I would do very well working in the community.

Internships can be helpful or irrelevant. I once held an internship at the District County Courthouse where I simply sat in court for six hours each day. I had no other work to do. People were always friendly and interacted with me, but when I would ask my boss for a task she simply shrugged her shoulders and said go to court. That was a very boring month in my life. However, it was an eye opening experience for me because I was able to narrow my focus. I knew I wanted to practice law, but I realized very quickly that being a public defender simply wasn't for me.

I have held several internships that have impacted the way I view the world. Each time I worked for Legal Aid, I was able to create impactful relationships, not only with my supervisors, but also with the people I helped. I listened to amazing stories, cleaned criminal records, and made friends with people I had met only minutes before. Internships have the ability to be impactful, so choose wisely. The skills you gain during your internship can have real life value. I learned how to use criminal databases, which is something I will use throughout my career. I also learned some legal jargon that will be helpful for me as I begin reading complicated briefs explaining the law.

Most people hold internships in the summer. You have to apply early! The positions will already be filled by, at the latest, April. Internships are all about taking the initiative and demonstrating a commitment to the organization. I didn't always get the internships I applied for and I got several "no's" before I got a "yes." Sometimes, you have to make positions for yourself. Internships are not always readily available and it may be very difficult to find the perfect fit. Often times, simply reaching out and expressing your interest can lead to opportunities. If you are passionate about a particular issue, simply highlighting your work ethic, how you will bring value to the company, and being personable can lead to an open door. The process can be long, but trust that with time, the right internship will work out.

Our Two Cents

➤ Internships can be completed during any year during your college journey. Most students complete one or two internships during their sophomore and junior summers.

➤ Internships can be unpaid, paid, or can give you class credit.

➤ Internships can also be completed during the semester, but in my eyes that's more of a part-time job.

➤ Most colleges or universities have internship and job fairs during the fall and spring semesters.

➤ Believe it or not, most companies are extremely excited to hire young college students, so smile big when you have opportunities to impress an employer (networking).

➤ You can't fail. Internships are meant for students who want to experience a career field.

➤ You can gain a full-time job from an internship. Most companies hire interns in the hopes of recruiting you when you graduate. If you perform well enough, companies might offer you a full-time job.

➤ Make the most of every second you have during your internship. There will be times during your internship that you will have the opportunity to network with individuals at senior and executive levels in the company.

➤ Don't forget your business cards!

CHAPTER 21

Grad School

"I applied to nine different law schools."

S: When thinking about graduate or professional school, there should be one question that guides your decision: Do you really need the additional degree to do what you ultimately want to accomplish?

My advice would be to go to the career counseling center, talk to a professor or professional in the field, or to research intensely exactly what the advanced degree offers and how it will be able to aid you later in life. Graduate school can affect long-term professional goals. It has the ability to shape and narrow your interest in a particular field. For example, if you go to graduate school to study molecular biology, you will probably only find yourself in a job that focuses on that particular topic. However, graduate programs also open the doors for higher paying, and more intensive opportunities.

There are two ways to go about graduate school applications and preparation. You can either continue on to grad school after you receive your undergraduate degree, or you can take some time off from school and work in your field of study for the experience. Then, apply for grad school when you're ready. This would allow you to save some money, pay off student loans and get to know if grad school is the right choice.

I chose to begin grad school the fall following my undergraduate graduation. I made this decision because I planned ahead. I laid out a timeline when I was a first-year student and stuck to it. Prepping for graduate or professional school doesn't start your senior year, it begins early on.

A: I didn't apply or plan to go to grad school following undergrad, but I can reassure you that prepping for anything post-grad doesn't begin your senior year. Setting goals before you get to college is so pertinent to the college experience and where you will land once you graduate.

S: It is important to investigate the process of applying to grad school.

Graduate schools look for a variety of different things in applicants. Research your school, understand the criteria, and make sure you're interested in the values a particular school will offer. You may be incredibly qualified for a school, but still get rejected. The schools are based off of peer applications and varying baselines. However, it goes a long way to connect with the school through some form or fashion beforehand. It demonstrates an interest in the school and puts you on the admission radar. I connected with a variety of programs before applying. I talked to admissions officers and attended online seminars. It was a great way for me to learn more about the programs and I was able to make connections to help me through the application process.

Depending on what program you choose, you'll have to take a standardized test. Most programs have different requirements. For example, medical, law, and business administration programs all require different tests. These tests can be difficult and aren't the sort of tests where you can study the night before. They require months of preparation and patience.

Once you are satisfied with your scores (btw, you may have to take the test several times), you will then apply to grad school. This will require you to finalize your resume, write personal essays, get letters of recommendation and wait patiently. It is a lot of work. After applying, it can take MONTHS to hear back. I heard back from some schools in less than three days and others I had to wait seven months. The process is long and exhausting to say the least.

One of the most important things I learned is that graduate school is expensive! It was shocking to me to recognize that my options for graduate school were, at a minimum, double my undergraduate degree. It is important to apply for every scholarship possible and understand all financial options before committing to a program.

I applied to nine different law schools. I heard my

first 'no' three days after I sent in the application. The admissions office looked at my test scores and said, 'no way.' It was a stretch for me to get into that particular school, but the rejection letter didn't hurt any less. I felt defeated. A few weeks later my second "no" came, then my third, then my forth. I had put so much hard work into applications and so much time into the process. At that point, I was disappointed and discouraged.

However, I didn't give up, and I was determined to stay positive. Eventually, I was accepted into my first law school, and then a few more. After some thought, I decided to accept my admission to The Norman Adrian Wiggins School of Law at Campbell University.

Our Two Cents

➤ Plan ahead - you can't decide to go to graduate school three weeks before the application is due.

➤ Ask for advice! Use your resources on campus. Professors, mentors, career counselors, and others are here to help you.

➤ Do your research. Graduate school is expensive, so you want to be sure that the program you're applying to actually fits what you want to do. You will need to research everything!

➤ Be positive, and don't get discouraged! Focus on your goals.

CHAPTER 22

A Sneak Peak

"Spice it up"

A: When I first started this author journey, I was 18 years old and I thought I was 10 foot tall and bulletproof. It's safe to say that I'm an old man now (maybe not entirely), but seeing as I graduated college three years ago, the 'real world' seems more of a norm now.

The whole 'real world' or life after college thing is much different. There's no pep rally when you arrive in your first apartment after college, there's no class schedule, and there's no college dining plan. In fact, there's a ton of differences. Since I made the most of my college experience, I landed a job, which in turn put a few quarters in my pocket. I still remember my first paycheck! I thought I had just become a millionaire, as I went to one of the fanciest restaurants and spent over $100 on a meal. Safe to say, I haven't been back to that restaurant.

For most of you, the transition from high school to college will either happen very soon or has happened within the last few months. The transition is exciting and nerve-racking all at the same time. You're leaving a place that you've most likely spent the majority of your life. You leave your friends that are your 'besties' to move to a place you know very little people. And the transition from college to the real world isn't much different. Except this time, you've probably gained deeper relationships with the friends you've made over the last four years, and the term 'bestie' turns into friends you'll have for a lifetime.

As you can imagine, the transition can be just as difficult, but just as exciting. When I was a senior in college, I was ready for a new chapter, but I wasn't ready to leave the people that had become so important to me. They make airports for a reason though, and my friends have never turned me down when I've needed a couch to lay my head on.

I graduated from college in May of 2016, and began working in July of 2016. Some of my friends elected to take more time before starting work and took a Euro-Trip or some other trip and that seemed to be the way to do it. I would've joined those folks in traveling across Europe, but it's hard to travel when you can't afford the plane ticket. So, I elected to spend more time with my family before moving to my first city after college, Charlotte, NC.

When looking at the beginning of the **real world** experience, there are a few big topics that come to mind. Below you'll see how I dealt with them and lessons learned:

Budgeting & Planning Finances

Since I was a business major, this skill came easily for me. I strongly encourage any new graduate to create a budget and track how you spend your money. There are many apps out there that help you keep a budget automatically like *Mint*, but I created my own spreadsheet right when I grad-uated. This budget/spending tracker has allowed me to see how much money I spend, save, and more importantly, where I spend my money. As someone who is not a huge shopper, most of my money is spent on food and travel.

My friends have joked with me and say I have tracked everything I have ever spent, which isn't entirely false, but I believe that if you keep track of it on a consistent basis, it creates discipline and also allows you to push to pay off your debts faster.

One last thing regarding finances when you grad-uate… if your employer offers a 401k plan, do it! Don't delay setting yourself up for retirement. No matter how small your contribution, it will make a world of differ-ence when you reach the golden age.

Dining & Drinking

This is definitely one area I haven't mastered, but to me, it's the most enjoyable. One of my favorite things about having an income is being able to try new foods and restaurants. Now, I will admit, I probably eat out more than I should, but I've never been one to love cooking. I have many friends who are experts at meal prepping and spend loads more than I do each month on that expense line item. I use eating as a way to build relationships. Since I have lots of friends that I don't work with, grabbing dinner or lunch on a Saturday is the best way to stay in touch.

If you read my previous book you know that drinking only became something I did during my senior year of college. Even though I have drunk more alcohol than I did in my college years, I still hold the same opinion on the subject. Alcohol has made me do silly things, sometimes I have drunk too much, but it still hasn't done anything magical for me as far as success goes.

Spicing it up

Like most stages in life, you'll get in a routine. You'll wake up early, go to work (or grad school), come home, eat, maybe exercise, and do it again. One of my biggest pieces of advice when it comes to transitioning to the **real world** is to spice it up. Make sure that you're staying grounded. If you have a faith, keep it at the center. If you have excess money, donate it, and get involved with that charity or non-profit. Exercise regularly, join a kickball team or a sport you enjoy. Make new friends through your friends. I didn't work for a company that had a lot of young people, but thoroughly enjoyed hanging out with my friend's work friends.

Independence, for real

One last thing that I believe is the most important part of making it to the **real world** is that college, in most situations, doesn't give you true independence. True independence comes when you're paying for your own phone bill, rent, food, insurance, you name it. True independence for me was when I graduated college. When I no longer had to depend on my parents for financial needs. Yes, I still rely on my parents for emotional support, and if they want to take me to dinner, I welcome it. Independence as I define it can be exciting and scary. You can't just miss work or not go grocery shopping, you never know when you'll need toilet paper. You have to take care of you when you're truly independent. You'll learn more about yourself while figuring this out than in any other part of your life.

I don't want you to think that college isn't a place that gives you true independence because I had friends who paid for 100% of their college experience. Those friends and students become independent the day they graduate high school. Most of you will become independent a few years after graduation. If you've truly made the most of your college experience, independence will come easier to you than your peers. The little things you do such as managing your time efficiently, meeting professors during office hours, and staying involved on campus throughout your four years, will all pay dividends as you close the college chapter in your life and you move onto the next.

My two cents

➤ It's never too early to start planning for your life after college. Polish that resume baby!

➤ Whatever life stage you're in, never be afraid to spice it up.

➤ Money creates more freedom, don't forget that life is all about choices, make great choices with your money.

➤ Independence is awesome. Make the most of college so you can make your mark on this world.

➤ Get off your parent's phone bill!

CHAPTER 23

Final Thoughts

"The ceiling is the roof!"

A: In 2017, arguably one of the greatest basketball players of all time screamed, "The ceiling is the roof" at the UNC vs Duke basketball game. Even though none of the fans in Chapel Hill understood Michael Jordan said that night, the crowd erupted in one of those ear deafening roars that was heard for miles. I think he meant to say, "the sky is the limit," but nobody argues with MJ (aka the G.O.A.T.), especially Tar Heel basketball fans. The Tar Heels went on to win the National Championship that year, and the Jordan Brand made a fortunate off of that simple five-word phrase.

In a lot of ways, I hope our book has had the same effect on you as Michael Jordan's speech did that night. No, we're not billion-dollar athletes - we're just kids. At one point, we were an eager high school graduate that couldn't wait to tackle college. We packed our bags, walked into our first dorm, and were determined to make a difference on our university's campus.

As you begin this journey, remember that college wasn't easy for us and it won't be easy for you. However, we guarantee if you listen to our advice, you too will be a *National Champion* and a college graduate that made the most of their four-year journey.

Never forget where you're from, or who you are. College won't be the best four years of your life, but the most unique. Every day is a new day to meet someone new, make an impact, and a difference. The sky really is the limit, or you can say it like MJ, "the ceiling is the roof!"

We'll leave you with our top pieces of advice from the year we graduated. College is all about the choices you make and the people you impact. Go get em!

SAVANNAH'S TOP 19

- Call home.
- Meet your neighbors.
- Go to sporting events.
- Prioritize school.
- Join organizations.
- Play an intramural (even if you aren't athletic).
- Make time for friends who you don't see everyday.
- Engage in campus traditions.
- Bring duct tape.
- Find a parking spot.
- Try different foods.
- Study abroad.
- Fail early.
- Do class readings.
- Take at least one class outside your comfort zone.
- Give back.
- Don't skip breakfast.
- Everything will be fine.
- Have fun! Enjoy your experience- you will never have one quite like it again.

AUSTIN'S TOP 16

- ➤ Make the most of your college experience. Make the most of every second. Make the most of your friendships. Time in college flies by, don't waste a second.
- ➤ Try everything possible. College is a testing ground; failure isn't really failure when you learn something. Get out there and try it all!
- ➤ Love your school! I can't say this enough. Show your school spirit every time you get a chance.
- ➤ Start now! Your resume, job application, and next chapter begins the day you move into college.
- ➤ Become a doer. Do things in college; don't just talk about doing them.
- ➤ Stay balanced. An unbalanced college career can be disastrous.
- ➤ Pray continuously and have faith.
- ➤ Grades are grades. Don't fret over a bad grade. It happens.
- ➤ Play intramurals, even if you're not athletic.
- ➤ Study abroad and travel when possible!
- ➤ Serve your college community! We all have our place to serve. Find that place early in your career.
- ➤ Explore entrepreneurship. Remember, you don't have to be a business student to be bitten by the entrepreneurial bug.

- Find your passion by exploring unknown territories.
- Be proud of your roots! I'm from Valdese, North Carolina!
- Make goals, revise goals, make more goals, and then act on those goals! (Email me with your goal lists!)
- Reflect on your experience by blogging, talking to friends, and debriefing with your support group!
- If you don't remember anything from our book, please remember that college isn't the best four years of your life, but is the most unique years as a young person. Make the most of every second and don't be afraid to fail. College is a clean slate, and it's just waiting for someone like you to take advantage of all it has to offer.

ABOUT THE AUTHORS

Savannah Putnam is from Morganton, North Carolina, who graduated from University of North Carolina at Chapel Hill in 2019. Putnam is an active public servant, leader, and advocate. Putnam served as Student Body President of UNC-Chapel Hill from 2018-2019 and is a member of Alpha Chi Omega sorority. Savannah enjoys playing sports and spending time with friends and family. Savannah is going to Campbell University to pursue a law degree with hopes of also getting a Master of Public Administration. Her career ambitions are to work in the state of North Carolina in local government.

Austin Helms is an entrepredoer, and author that resides in Charlotte, NC. *Orientation to Graduation* (his first book) was aimed at making sure every student, no matter their background, income level, or hometown, made the most of their college experience. Helms is a small-town kid, with big time dreams. Helms graduated from UNC-Chapel Hill in 2016 and hasn't stopped moving since. Helms has also been known to live for the 'Oh My' Moments meaning he's ran with the bulls in Spain, driven solo across the US (9300 miles in 28 days), and helped grow a business from $0 to $5M in revenue in 18 months. Helms also enjoys speaking at high schools and colleges across the Southeast.

Contact Info:

Austin Helms
www.austinhelms.org
Email: austinhelms32@gmail.com
Phone: (828) 448-5521
@austinhelms32

Savannah Putnam
savananhputnam23@gmail.com

ACKNOWLEDGMENTS

They say it takes a village to raise a child, and it's safe to say, it takes a village to publish a book. We'd like to thank everyone that had a direct or indirect impact on the publishing of *Orientation to Graduation 2.0*.

This book wouldn't have been possible without the help of editors, designers, reviewers, teachers, parents, friends, and many more. Huge shout out to The University of North Carolina at Chapel Hill & the Burke County Public School system. Both places gave Savannah and I the opportunity to receive diplomas, and we'll be forever grateful.

Made in the USA
Middletown, DE
21 June 2019